"I Hid It In My Diaper!"

& Other Senior Stories!

JOEY EDMONDS
Author Of:

JOEY EDMONDS ~ *Claustrophobic*
&
FUN with *"Fears & Phobias"*

<u>R</u>   <u>U</u>
In this book?

"I Hid It In My Diaper!"

& Other Senior Stories!"

Copyright @ 2010 Joey Edmonds
All rights reserved

ISBN 978-0-615-36586-2

www.JoeyEdmondsSpeaker.com

joey@joeyedmondsspeaker.com

To the classiest, most honest and knowledgeable human I have ever met!

(Wife of 41 Years)

LYNN BILEK EDMONDS

Author of:

<u>I ONLY HAVE TROUBLE WITH PEOPLE…</u>

Author's Notes

I live in an area of Burbank, California Home of Toluca Townhouse #1 or # 2 or #3 or # 4 or # 5 or #6 or #7. Many of my complex dwellers are on social security and I am amazed at the tales these present & former actors, writers, artists producers, engineers, movie technicians, cinematographers, school teachers, mechanics, horse owners, soccer referees, musicians, and CIA agents have to share! The stories keep on coming!

More Author's Notes

Book #1 **Joey Edmonds ~ *Claustrophobic***

A personal exploration of being enclosed!

While writing book #1, I created a YOUTUBE site asking others to tell me their phobias. I received 100's of responses, but not one person offered their name. This secretive reaction convinced me to write Book #2, leading to the creation of my **"Fears & Phobias" FUN ~ Seminar Lecture** for Corporations & Colleges.

Book #2 ***FUN with "Fears & Phobias"***
What a delight to write. Dozens of musings providing a conduit to laugh while being affected by one or more of the topics.   R   U
                In this book?

More Author's Notes

Current Publication:
   Title Is A True Story

Lynn's dear friend Judie recently placed her mother into a nursing home and knowing that Lynn's mom spent her last few years in a home, Judie asked for advice. Lynn's advice? "Never leave any thing of value at the home!" This past year Judie found an oval framed picture of her parents and presented it to her mother reminding her to always place it in her chest of drawers after viewing. During her visit a few days later, Judie failed to locate the picture. When mom woke from her nap, Judie asked about the picture and mom whispered,

"I Hid It In My Diaper!"
Dedicated to: (Judie & Mom)

"I Hid It In My Diaper!"
& Other Senior Stories!

Grocery Store	11
Lincoln Park Zoo (Chicago)	12
Edmonds' Parties	14
Senior Golfers	18
Senior Soccer Referee	21
Reunions	25
Grand Kids	29
"Some Day"	31
Indiana Jones ~ Utah Jim	33
Harry Chapin	36
British Retirement	38
SENIOR JOKE	39
Cycling Senior	40
Telephones	41
Like Father ~ Like Son!	43
Walt Disney & Me!	45
I'm NOT a Fireman	52
UKULELE Birthdays	55
Senior Spacewalker	57
PICNIC ~ The Movie	59
The Blarney Stone	62
YO-YO World	69
Senior Group Moments	72

"I Hid It In My Diaper!"
& Other Senior Stories!

'THE BIG GUYS' ~ Johnny Carson 73
Ed McMahon 74
Carl Reiner 75
Jay Leno 76
Andy Kaufman 78
Red Skelton 80
David Frost 81
Merv Griffin 82
Candice Bergen 84
Chico & the Man 85
Jerry Seinfeld 86
Larry David 87
John Denver 88
Steve Allen 89
Jonathon Winters 90
Mike Douglas 92
H I M 97

GROCERY STORE!

I'm in a grocery store aisle searching for a can of chicken gravy. I walk the length of the aisle 3 times excusing myself to the other shoppers, and finally I loudly declare "I am searching for the gravy section, please let me know if you find it!" One lady releases a boisterous laugh and four others join in. I smile and give a silly shrug. A few moments later a voice shouts "Gravy is down here Sir… bottom shelf!" "Thank you" I shout back and make my way to the gravy shelf, grab a can and join the 10 items or less line behind the lady with the wild laugh. She turns to me and says "That's the first time I've ever laughed in a grocery store!" I nod and reply,

"Glad I could help!"

LINCOLN PARK ZOO

A friend of mine lives in Chicago and two or three times a week she visits her elderly father who lives across from the Lincoln Park Zoo. Fortunately (or maybe not), he is quite mobile. During a recent visit they decided to once again 'go to the zoo'. It was a mild spring day and they made their way to the tunnel on Lakeview and proceeded to the Monkey Habitat! After spending time watching the monkeys swing and back and forth, dad let it be known it was time to visit the bathroom. They arrived at the door marked MENS and as was their routine, she assured him she would wait for him by the door. After five minutes she opened the door and loudly announced "Woman in the Men's room"!

Boldly she entered and hanging on the sink was a sign: <u>Construction!</u> On the far side of the MENS room was a 'make shift' door thru which dad had exited and wandered off. It took only a few minutes to find him. When in doubt she learned, go to the monkey habitat. After escorting him back to his apartment, she drove home with no further oddities except as she entered her house the phone was ringing. She did answer to find it was a call from dad asking if she would be visiting today? Eventually Dad was transferred to a nursing home where he spent the next few years wandering and making life interesting for a cadre of nurses. (Chicago's Lincoln Park Zoo is a must 'visit' followed by a trek to Wrigley Field, Home of the Cubbies!)

EDMONDS' PARTIES

Parties at the Edmonds house have become legendary! Every three or four months my wife Lynn & I, brother and sister-in-law (the Medicare crew), menopausal single adults as well as thirty year olds (friends of kids Kate & Grant) appear at the front door and the party is on! Each guest is in some fashion connected to Show Business, which provides a wide range of 'peppered' and non-stop 'tart' responses during the evening. A variety of mystery games may be played or anything and everything 'wild' poker games may surface! Once a year a volleyball pool party erupts followed by charades, food and ill-advised tales from the past that are greeted by "Dad, we've heard that more than once!"

*

I truly enjoy retelling good stories. However, certain critics in the family have determined that many of my 'renderings' were not laced with humor even the first time……. blah, blah, blah !

    Super Bowls and other theme parties, i.e. Academy Awards, etc. are always fun. The annual Miss America Pageant was the latest excuse to party. Pageants are interesting because the party guests feel free to talk to the TV, creating an evening of reality TV. Early in the show each contestant tells her name and the state she represents. We get a chance to give a numerical score (1 thru 5) judging her speaking prowess (or lack thereof).
This year Miss South Carolina won in a landslide!

*

It wasn't the cute 'southern drawl' or the pretty face that gave her the speaking award, it was the entire sentence.

" My name is Jane Doe and I'm from South Carolina where it's against the law to keep a horse in your bath tub!"
Applause and 'high fives' for this lady! Swimsuits are next and each year Mary Lou, a friend of my daughter insists she could still compete! Mary Lou drinks… A lot! We men don't say much while the scantly clad ladies reveal most of their birthmarks! <u>It's FANTASY TIME for us!</u> Talent is next… The usual fare: ballet dancers (yes, more than one) piano players, baton twirlers, and singers. Singers including one lady whose first note was a high C…the defining moment of a 'one note singer'!

*

Often numbers from popular musicals are attempted and when presentations fall short of the mark, venom fills the room. One lady sang from Les Miserable and before she finished the first eight bars, a voice cried out…"She should have been shot at the Bastille!" So Bad! And So Funny! Eventually Miss Virginia was awarded the crown! We all drank to her AND to the up coming Academy Awards in just 7 weeks! (Go HURT LOCKER!) St. Patrick's day was next followed by Kate's birthday in March and this Author's on the first day in June!

Another successful and fun party with the EDMONDS!

SENIOR GOLFERS

During my freshmen year in high school, I bought a $10 dollar pass which allowed me to play unlimited rounds of golf Monday thru Friday. Except for six rain days, I played 36 holes every day. Sixty days later I shot par! Never again did I par a course. I played golf until my thirties when I became a Soccer Referee. I have fond memories of Thom Curley (my comedy partner) and me on dozens of golf courses while touring colleges those 14 years. Let me insert this: THOM CURLEY is <u>very</u> <u>funny</u>…always <u>very</u> <u>funny!</u> A particular incident is quite memorable. It was in South Carolina and the activity director (also named Tom minus the 'h'), made it possible for us to play nine holes. He said he would meet us later on the 5th tee.

As was our custom we played in shorts and shirtless. I guess Director Tom forgot to mention this was a very private course. We had the course to ourselves until we got to the 5th tee. Four very senior southern gentlemen in two carts pulled up and that's when the 'fun started'! It was the 300 pound golfer who started a vocal attack on us concerning our wardrobe that escalated when Thom realized this was going to be FUN! Sentences filled with adjectives were not recorded, but they should have been! At that moment Director Tom drove up and the sight of us in shorts and shirtless confronting the four members of the club, removed any dignity he might have had. They knew Director Tom and unleashed a tirade on him!

*

We decided we'd had enough golf so Thom drove toward the cart path and then stopped… After all those years together I knew he was not finished! Our new friends teed off one by one by one and finally it was the "Big Guys" turn to tee it up. He addressed the ball and at the top of his swing Curley screamed a loud and elongated <u>F O R E !</u> and off we went. The four of them were frantically shaking their fists and mouthing words we could only imagine. Word quickly made it's way back to Director Tom and I know he was secretly laughing, but this was the south in the 1970's and we were a couple of 'Yankees' a wee bit out of line! Director Tom still talks about the day Joey & Thom played golf at Winthrop University.

SENIOR SOCCER REFEREE

I often mention soccer because I have been a referee for 40 years and really do have fun running with the 12 or 14 year olds (boys or girls) in the middle of the field. The players (kids) are always terrific and to make sure the spectators get it, I walk to the touch lines on both sides of the field where 2 dozen canvas folding chairs are lined up in a perfect row giving comfort to parents and *their* parents. These games are truly for three generations of family. All become curious when referee Joey comes to visit. Like a coach talking to the players, I suggest to them "that if they really want their child or grandchild's team to win, they need to understand that coffee at halftime makes a happy referee!"

I quickly turn and jog to other side of the field. I then repeat the same spiel to the visiting team. At half time some years ago, the 3 of us referees were about to leave the field when a parent from each team greeted us holding a coffee container. Flashing a smile I clutched both cups and handed one to each assistant. I turned to each bench and instructed my assistants to raise their cup to the home team and then the visitors. I gave the soccer 'thumbs up' signal to both! I've learned that being 'old' and having a disarming smile, can be carte blanche for most any encounter. I'll never forget the game I refereed for son 'Grant's high school soccer team. It was family day and people of all ages filled the bleachers.

We waited, but the assigned officials failed to appear. I always keep my soccer equipment in the trunk of my car. Shoes, uniform, whistles, cards (which I rarely use). I warmed up stretching, running forward and backward, caring for the legs that have been my best friends these many thousands of miles, propelling me into correct positions to make my presence known to the players. The visitors scored in the first half. Then with 3 minutes remaining in the match, I whistled a foul resulting in a penalty kick for Grant's team. I observed all the players making sure they were out of the penalty area (box). I gave the ball to the kicker who I realized was Grant. He placed it on the penalty mark.
I'm thinking 'How wonderful is this!'

*

(Father/Referee) (Son/Player). I sharply blow the whistle and Grant boots it perfectly into the left upper corner of the net. Again I blow the whistle and signal NO GOAL! Problem… Three of Grant's teammates encroached, meaning they entered the penalty area prior to Grant's kick. Pointing to the PK mark I shout "RE KICK!" On my whistle Grant once again attempts the PK. This time it hits the crossbar and is booted out of danger by the opposing team. A minute later I gave 3 blasts of my whistle. Game Over! Walking toward the bleachers I knew there would be questions challenging my NO GOAL call. I placed myself in front of them and explained, "Folks, until the ball is kicked, only the kicker is allowed in the box." Grant later said, "Good call Ref!"

CLASS REUNIONS

There seem to be those who love to attend class reunions and before the evening is over they start planning for the next one. It's not good enough to hold a 10 year, 25 year or 50 year reunion. Their class should get together every 5 years or as the years go by, every 4 years maybe. I think the spouse of the invitee should be given more consideration. Perhaps the couple that fell in love during their school days would equally enjoy reliving the past and catching up on the present with their old classmates. But I dare say, those couples are few and far between if indeed they are still together. The spouse who didn't share all those experiences can't honestly be that interested. He/she didn't fall in love with a teenager.

✱

The spouse met and married an individual farther along in life and hopefully more mature. Your mate in high school would be a stranger to you. You are placed in a situation from another dimension, another world, another time. You are hearing things you can never truly understand.
You were not there. How can others' reminiscences make for a comfortable evening? Anyway, I assume many just smile, while gritting their teeth, and try to be as cordial as possible. And say to their partner afterward, "You owe me one."

"I ONLY HAVE TROUBLE WITH PEOPLE...who relish reunions".
Used with permission from Author:
Lynn Bilek Edmonds!

Senior Story from Friends: #1

Entering the banquet hall for my 40th high school class reunion, I experienced an adrenalin rush that I last felt 40 years ago leading my teammates onto the field for our senior homecoming football game. I avoided previous reunions acquiescing to my wife Sheryl's desire not to attend as she was not part of my class, school, city or state! Her mantra that evening was 'keep my glass full'! There were dozens and dozens and dozens of classmates already in the hall when we made our way to the registration desk for our badges and 'goodie bag'. We entered the big hall and immediately a small group welcomed us. Who ever invented name badges, I thank you! After 40 years, not many classmates looked familiar.

*

Sheryl was terrific! Of course my refilling her glass probably helped. The reunion was a wonderful reminder of the fun I had in high school and because I was quite the 'jock' back then, most people remembered me. Apparently I had too much fun during those high school years. Numerous stories about me on and off the football field were tossed about and Sheryl just kept sipping and smiling. Late in the evening as we were about to leave, Sheryl visited the ladies room and I wandered over to a table that displayed wallet sized pictures of my class. After searching the table for my picture it hit me! These classmates were no longer with us!

WHOA!

GRAND KIDS

There is a special bond between grand parent and grandchild. We have all heard the statement "being a grandparent is the best job in the world, we don't have to take them home with us. We don't have our naps interrupted and if there is a problem, mom (or dad) will be home soon". Of course no grandparent would ever say that in front of the precious little one(s); however, mom and dad have been known to exclaim, "Are you sure you don't want to go home with grandma (pa)?" There are so many first times. Birthdays, holidays, school events, soccer games, dances, music recitals, graduations, etc. When introducing a friend it seems natural for a grandchild to exclaim. "This is my grandma or this is my grandpa pa!" Somehow it's not as easy to say, "This is my mom & dad".

*

Grandparents are able to give full attention as opposed to what they get in a house filled with 6 siblings and 2 parents. Name a kid that does not like a grand parent! I remember often visiting my grandpa when I was still in grade school, and listening to him telling me stories I have long ago forgotten. He always had a mouthful of tobacco which created juice which he spat into the spittoon on the floor adjacent to the RCA Victor Radio.

It is always fun watching a child and grandparent in public. Seniors reaching out and grasping a child's hand, leading them out of the mall parking lot. Little gifts of ice cream, miniature stuffed cats or dogs, a plastic ball, always laughter! Except when they <u>pass!</u> Another first!

VERY SAD

"SOME DAY"

**#1 - I'm in a grocery store check out line and a middle aged lady in front of me can barely contain her frustration because a senior lady in front of her continues to search her purse for change in the amount of 56 cents. Finally the 56 cents is handed to the clerk and the lady in front of me gives me that look of indignation and I point to myself …
and then point to her and whisper…**

~ **"SOME DAY!"** ~

It took a few seconds…but she got it, and smiled!

#2 – I'm an altar boy in sixth grade and a fellow altar boy thought it was fun to nudge the throat of older people with the communion plate which prevents the 'host' from falling to the floor.

*

The priest was very observant and later in the vestibule, chastised my fellow altar boy with some strong comments regarding his lack of caring for people! He used the phrase...

~ "SOME DAY!" ~

Hopefully my fellow altar boy got the message! The term "SOME DAY!" can and should be thought frequently. It is usually in an awkward moment that age, and physical, or mental differences frustrate us. One of us is happy ...we're still young!   ...but,
~ "SOME DAY!" ~

As I age I often think of those words, and now a new one... Tomorrow!?!

INDIANA JONES ~ UTAH JIM!

Neighbor Jim is one of those individuals who can pretty much repair anything. He is also an avid sportsman whether it be fishing, trap shooting, or deer hunting. He has done it all and continues to join his Oklahoma buddies each October in Southeast Utah, where they erect two huge tents, creating many of the amenities of home for 10 days in the Devil's Canyon / Blue Mountain range. Now in his mid-sixties, he continues to hunt deer. Watching and listening to him tell of his experience in Devil's Canyon a few years past, was like listening to a child relating his or her scary first ride on a roller coaster! Exciting! "One time I said to my partners, I'm going to head down the Canyon and maybe I'll see a deer!

I grabbed my rifle and started strolling down the Canyon passing boulders the size of a Volkswagen or small truck. Some as big as a house. I got down to this one little area and I couldn't quite see further down the canyon as much as I wanted to, so I spotted this large egg shaped boulder and I stepped on it and walked out to the edge and damn if it didn't start to tilt down, and before I could step back it was already down to the point that I had to do something. So I jumped in front of it and threw my rifle off to the side, and I'll be damned… I started rolling like I was inside of a carpet and every time I looked up that boulder was tumbling after me and it crossed my mind that my hunting days were over. I was managing to just stay ahead of it.

During one revolution of my rolling, I spotted another enormous boulder and rolled to the base of it which prevented the 'attacking egg' boulder from making any sort of contact with me. It did make contact with the immovable boulder and careened out of control to the bottom of Devil's Canyon! There I was lying in the crevice that saved me. When I extracted myself, both hands were scraped and bleeding. Locating my rifle I made my way back to our campground and when my buddies saw me they immediately worked on my hands, cleaning and bandaging them. After a couple of 'shots of J.D. I told them my story. They then told me when I lumbered into camp and they saw my ashen color, they were ready to call the medics!"

HARRY CHAPIN

E & C's (EDMONDS & CURLEY'S) first of many concerts with Harry Chapin was at Western Illinois University in the early 70's. The gymnasium was packed and once we finally convinced security we were part of the show, they led us to a locker room where the band members were tuning their instruments, smoking, and drinking water from plastic cups.

(NO WATER BOTTLES in the 70's) We said our hello's to all except Harry, who I found a few moments later as I pushed open the door of a bathroom stall! "Excuse me" I murmured looking directly at Harry. He said, "I was just leaving." We both chuckled. Later Harry shook hands with Thom telling him "I already met your partner!"

*

During our performance, it was exciting to see Harry in the wings stage left, laughing and obviously enjoying the physicality and Thom's sound effects in our show. We walked off stage and he greeted us with a big smile and said "We'll be working together many times!" And we did! We were told that Harry never had used an opening act before. After his performance we knew why. What a PARTY! Who else but Harry could sing 15-20 songs, 5 minutes or longer and play with the audience for two hours. He was a magnet for people. Women and men loved him. Often he performed solo, donating hundreds of thousands of dollars to the Harry Chapin Foundation!

Harry Chapin would be 68 this year!

BRITISH RETIREMENT

A relative traveling in England sent me this 'ditty'. A rather adventurous Senior Brit recently failed to show up for his post at the London Zoo. His job was to collect monies from vehicles' owners at parking lots adjacent to the entrance gates. Autos were 1 British pound and buses 2 British pounds. They paid their money to 'John Doe' who gave them a parking ticket and welcomed them to the zoo! He had serviced thousands of zoo visitors for over 20 years and when he failed to show up it caused quite a stir. Apparently 'John Doe' had created his own 'official booth' and with his own 'official' uniform had bilked the Zoo of seven million British pounds.

SENIOR JOKE

Mable: "Fred, I have a taste for ice cream, would you like some?"

Fred: "Yes dear…could you add some chocolate syrup…and a few sprinkles…and a little Reddi Whip!"

Mable: "Yes dear."

(15 minutes later)

Mable: "Here's your scrambled eggs!"

Fred: ….."Where's the bacon?"

Author's note: In the spirit of decency & class, no other Senior Jokes have been included in this book! Create your Own!

CYCLING SENIOR

I have a neighbor who works the night shift in a hospital. He goes home, sleeps and often when he wakes, he dons his riding gear and off he cycles to one of many locations. He is not yet a senior like 'yours truly', but one of his rider acquaintances has been a senior for many years. Six days each week this 84 year old gentleman packs a lunch and rides his bike from Burbank to the ROSE BOWL near Pasadena. The distance is 10 miles. He has lunch and returns to Burbank. The 20 miles he rides is NOT like 20 miles in Iowa… California is covered with hills. As Roy Rogers sang for many years,

HAPPY TRAILS TO YOU!

TELEPHONES

1.800.555.1212

Dial this number and you will hear the recorded message "Toll free directory assistance powered by ****! Please say the listing you want!" Almost any person or business will be provided. As a 16 year old, my aunt Rita worked as a telephone operator and continued working with the phone company for the next 50 years. I remember being permitted to 'see' where Rita worked one time only. Rules did not permit outsiders in the work place but somehow I got in. What I saw was a large narrow room, each side containing hundreds of female receptacles which allowed a male connection at the end of a 4 foot cord, to be inserted providing a pathway for sound!

*

One side of the described wall contained the 'Stanley' numbers and the parallel wall contained 'Blackhawk' numbers. In addition the 'rural' phone numbers had a different prefix…Alden ####. The Alden numbers were on a different floor. Primitive? Oh YES! 60 years have passed since I picked up my family phone and heard an operator say… "Number please." I would reply: "Stanley ####, or Blackhawk ####, or Alden ####." One time I picked up the phone (only method to connect with an operator) and continued picking up and hanging up until aunt Rita's voice resonated "Number Please?" I replied, "Rita, it's Joey…" Pause… "Number Please."

She took her job <u>so</u> seriously.

LIKE FATHER ~ LIKE SON!

In their late sixties my dad, mom and mom's sister traveled extensively. Mom and sis shared the driving while dad sat in the roomy back seat. One day after eating lunch, dad took his usual digestive walk around the massive restaurant parking lot. After 10 minutes or so he made his way to the car, opened the back door and got in. The driver and passenger in the front turned and gazed at the senior citizen in the back seat who with hands clasped on his lap, had already closed his eyes for his post lunch nap! ...
    YEP.....Wrong car!
Two years ago Lynn & I flew to Mitchell field in Milwaukee to attend my 50th Oshkosh High School class reunion.
I rented a bright red thunderbird and headed north.

*

After two wonderful days visiting with classmates, we headed back to Milwaukee with a stop for lunch at a restaurant named Bublitz's. I parked my bright red car in an almost empty parking lot. After a leisurely lunch we made our way to the parking lot, which was now pretty much full. It is amazing how a bright red car can be spotted even in a full parking lot. While Lynn stood waiting by the front passenger door, I pressed the open door buttons. Nothing! "Lynn, where are my glasses?" While she 'dug' for the glasses in her purse, I tried the actual key and attempted to insert it into the key hole.

 A blaring siren forced me to cover my ears. A rather 'portly' lady came running out asking "Why are you trying to break into my bright red car?"   Whoops!

WALT DISNEY & ME!

<u>ME</u> is NOT Joey Edmonds…<u>ME</u> is a 76 year old man who spent 30 years with Walt Disney Studios from 1963 to 1993.

<u>I'll let him tell his own story:</u>

On November 18, 1963 I was hired for a one day call at Disney Studios. I was on the set of "Wonderful World of Color" and Walt Disney came off the set to a long line of animators, writers, editors, etc. who were waiting to talk with him. I was to move a large light to the far side of the set and in order to do that I needed to get through this long line. I reached out and touched Mr. Disney on the shoulder and said "Excuse me, Mr. Disney" and in a voice loud enough to stop 60 people on the set in their tracks, he said "What did you just say?"

As the blood rose up through my neck into my head, I said "I'm sorry but I have to get this through." and he said, "No, no, no, I understand that. You're new aren't you?" and I said "My first day sir." He said "What's your name?" I figured I'm a dead man and I'll never work here again! I said "My name is Herb, Herb Hughes." He said "Well what do your friends call you"? "They call me Herbie sir." He said "Well Herbie, let me explain something to you. In this organization there are only two Misters. Mr. Toad & Mr. Lincoln. Everybody else goes by their first name. My name's Walt. You call me Walt and I'll call you Herbie and we'll be friends." I said "Okay Mr. Disney!" Everyone laughed nervously and the line opened and I pushed my light through.

A week later I was given a union call back at Disney Studios for a one day job and again I was involved with Walt. I was assigned a lighting project that he was overseeing and there was discussion concerning synchronism of sound with film and I mentioned my father back in Nebraska who was very interested in that subject. Shortly thereafter I was offered a permanent position at Disney Studios. One thing led to another and I spent the next few years chatting with Walt from time to time. It was not uncommon for Walt to walk up beside me on the back lot and say "Well Herbie, what are you guys doing today?" My response usually was, "Walt, you own this place, why are you asking me?" His response gave an insight to the man…

…"Your job is more important than mine around here so I ask people like you so that I know what's going on!"

Over the following years we became quite close. One particular day on the Western Street, we talked about all the buildings and their titles. An award winning set designer nominated for many academy awards was John Mansbridge and his building was 'MANSBRIDGE MERCANTILE'. Ron Miller was his son-in-law and there was 'MILLER FEED & GRAIN', and a lady who ultimately became my office manager when I made my final assent into the top category of my trade, was an English war bride by the name of Blanche Teller and on the back lot there was a building named 'TELLER JEWELRY'.

*

Almost every back lot building was so named! One day standing in the middle of Western Street talking to Walt I said,
"Walt will there ever come a day when I can get my name on something around here?" He said "Herbie, I promise you that I'll put your name on something!" That's the true story. I made no claim then, never have, never will. That was a special moment in my life I shared with Walt Disney. On another occasion when I was parking on the lot, I said to Walt …"Would you like to see the fastest Volkswagen in California?" Of course he was agreeable. After showing Walt my VW, I explained that my father, with major alterations, converted a large military surplus vacuum cleaner into the only turbo charged 1956 VW in the world!

"HERBIE The Love Bug" Movie!

On Saturday before the big race sequence on Sunday, there was a race held which was choreographed so that HERBIE would win. Now understand, he was up against the Jaguars, the Ferraris, Austin Martins & a number of other English and Italian sports cars. So in real life HERBIE would not have stood a chance, but we're talking movies here! So anyway, all the other drivers had to drive so HERBIE looked like he was winning. I can tell you for a fact, there was a super 1600 CC Porsche engine in HERBIE during that racing sequence in the movie. Later on they built a car that split in half and continued to go forward!

They built another one that had so much <u>lead</u> in the back end that when you touched the accelerator it went into an instant wheelie! There were other specialty cars that they cut and modified to make HERBIE appear to have it's own spirit and life on board. So that's pretty much the story how HERBIE got his name. I claim it, I don't want to profit by it, but Walt did say that to me. Walt passed away in 1966 and "HERBIE the Love Bug" was made in 1967.

<u>AUTHOR'S NOTE:</u> Taping Herbie Hughes for this interview could have lasted an entire day. His knowledge of the many facets in the industry during his time spent with the Disney Studio is amazing. It was a pleasure writing this chapter!

I'M NOT A FIREMAN!

A couple of years back I met a rather shy and gentle soul who had just moved into the neighborhood. As I got to know him he continued to be a gentle soul. SHY? Not so much! Gregarious? Oh Yeah! He and his Canadian wife make the perfect couple. Always walking their little dog or riding their bikes or golfing. After a few conversations and many laughs, I asked if he still worked and he said "I'm retired." (I have asked the next question 100's of times and it's exciting to imagine the forth coming answer!) Retired from what? And he replied "Police Officer! I was a Cop!" I'm confident he noticed my rather large smile because he was already laughing! "Really" said I. "Yes" said he.

I envisioned 'officer' as I now call him, making an arrest and the bad guy on the ground rolling with laughter.

After reading my first book dealing with *Claustrophobia*, 'officer' admitted to having a fear of heights and yes, he had a story. It seems there were 'bad guys' making their way into buildings and removing what was not theirs to remove. How did they get into the buildings? Through the roof! So 'officer' and his supervisor were assigned to check out a particular location. A hook and ladder fire truck was brought in and a ladder was extended upward to the third floor roof. 'Officer' was instructed to climb the ladder and check it out! 'Officer' made it quite clear that he did not do ladders.

*

With protestations such as "I'm not climbing a ladder… firemen climb ladders…I'm not a fireman!" The supervisor was not forgiving! "Firemen are not trained to capture bad guys…Get up that ladder!" So after securing his keys in his belt buckle, he slowly made his way up the ladder to the roof. He gave a quick scan of the roof with his flashlight and then *froze*! His fear of heights came into the equation and he shouted down to his supervisor, "I need some help up here!" "Don't look down!" was the supervisor's response. Finally 'officer' placed his feet back on the ground and removed his safety belt and discovered that his keys had fallen from his belt on the roof! Yes, he had to climb up one more time!

UKULELE BIRTHDAYS

On my 14th birthday I was given a gift that changed my life. A <u>ukulele!</u> I quickly learned to play it and now had an instrument to accompany my singing. In college I advanced to guitar & 5-string banjo, forming a folk singing trio: The TRI-ADDS! (Listen on YOUTUBE)

But I digress…

That 'uke' is still with me and is played each time my brothers (2), sisters (3), brother-in-laws (2), and sister-in-laws (2) turn another year older. On each of those special days I grab my 'uke' and Lynn joins me next to the speaker phone. I strum the 'uke' once to establish the 'key' and then dial the birthday girl or boy's number and wait for their "HELLO"! Immediately we break into our birthday duet. Happy Birthday, etc.etc.

*

We then wait for applause or a thank you. Each recipient of our musical offering thanks us in their own unique way. One brother (who I think might be in a witness protection program) has caller I. D. and each birthday answers the phone "I hope you don't have the 'uke'!" Before he can finish his sentence, we're already singing "Happy Birthday to you, etc" and each year we hear "OH JEEZ !" This year my middle sister's birthday call was most unusual. We dialed and it took 6 rings before "Hello" "Happy Birthday to you, etc., etc" Pause, then slowly "That was beautiful, but it's not my birthday!" My <u>Dialing Error</u> made an 87 year old lady very happy! After I hung up, we could not harness our laughter!

        Such an appreciative lady!

SENIOR SPACEWALKER!

Sometimes I'm not so bright and advanced age seems to compound this condition. I'm at work in the warehouse and anxious to leave for an important function. The loading dock seems to be the quickest way out. They call it a 'Loading Dock'... operative term, <u>'Dock'</u>. If the 'dock' was at ground level, they might call it a 'Loading Flat' or just 'Loading Area'! No, it's a 'Dock'!

    You may not know this, but to keep rain and direct sun light out of these open dock areas, warehouses have overlapping translucent strips of plastic hanging across the opening. Finally work is finished and I briskly walk toward the 'Loading Dock'.

*

Not unlike Moses parting the Red Sea, I parted the translucent strips and in full stride walk directly into 'Space' some five (5) feet above the ground.

It's surprising the things you can say to yourself in a split second of stupidity! It goes something like this, but to keep it "clean" there are some serious omissions. "DAH! You Idiot! You're DEFINITELY about to experience EXTREME pain and soon!" Luckily for me, I lived to tell this story.

Author of this story has been involved with CAAF (Children Affected by Aids Foundation) for many, many years. A great guy, but Clumsy! (not true)

PICNIC ~ The Movie!

When we moved to California my first conversation was with Roger, a neighbor in my townhouse complex. The usual banter of root exploration revealed we had both lived in Chicago for many years. I learned he was a native of Burbank. I learned the driveway we were standing on used to be an expansive field where movies were filmed. As a teenager in the fifties he lived a few blocks away on Woodland Avenue where a long fence separated his neighborhood from the field. He confessed that he frequently climbed that fence to watch the making of movies and mentioned that because of the variance of sunshine and clouds, most movies were filmed at night when lighting could be controlled.

Roger had years of memories stored away and realizing he was conversing with someone who really wanted him to share those memories, continued talking. "The main street for cars going north & south was Pass Avenue and because of beeping car horns, numerous scenes were filmed again & again. Studios would hire people to hold up signs informing drivers "SILENCE- FILMING IN PROGRESS!" He told of many Cowboy & Indian movies and hundreds of horses galloping on this field. I asked him what was the most memorable movie he observed being filmed and without missing a beat he said, "PICNIC" with William Holden, and Kim Novak in 1955. The transformation of that field into a park surrounding a large pond was amazing."

*

Roger said that even from his home a football field away, he knew there was something special happening to the field. A few days later he was able to get within viewing distance and there it was! Seeing a pond with a dock reaching from the center of the pond back to the shore was surreal. Filming was done at night which made it easy for Roger and a friend to find a 'spot' and observe many of the dance scenes. He remembers William Holden being extremely irritated after the 6th or 7th take, however, that scene was the most erotic dance routine ever filmed!

A MASTERFUL SCENE!

To view Go to Google… PICNIC!

THE BLARNEY STONE!

Senior Story from Friends: #2

Our plane did not arrive in Dublin until 10 pm and because we were 'tardy' and this was the first day of IRISH Fest, our rooms were gone. This happened 40 years ago and was a prelude to the hours we were to spend in Ireland. The night manager did his best to provide us with two beds (not yet married). I had a lower bunk on the 2nd floor with 3 other 'lost souls' while fiancé slept on a large couch located on the stage of a small theater connected to the PUB which we visited immediately before 'last call'. We each downed a 'pint' and called it a night. The night manager assured us everything would be fine and it was! The next morning I was roused by one of my bunk mates and joined 'mystery wife' as the other guys called her, for breakfast.

We both worked for the United States Government (I was a C.I.A. agent and she worked for the State Department) and our tours of duty in Vienna, Austria had ended. In a few days we would debark from South Hampton, England on a ship and a few days later savor the Statue of Liberty in New York Harbor. Our plan today was to visit the city of CORK, the birthplace of my ancestors and of course kiss the *Blarney Stone*!

    We ate and within the hour we were on the train to CORK. Gorgeous was the term we use for the countryside…it was green, green and misty green! Beautiful! Upon our arrival we met an old gent (we met a variety of old gents on this one day journey) who gladly shared his knowledge of travel to BLARNEY!

We were instructed to board the next Narrow Gauge to BLARNEY. (Narrow Gauge trains are unique. The rails are closer together and each compartment is entered from an outside door.) He told us each city had a marker and to get off at the 3rd stop. Off we went in our own little cubicle and soon a marker for the 1st stop appeared. Twenty minutes later we were off again still amazed at the misty and green countryside. Soon the 2nd stop marker came into sight. We watched as one passenger departed and appeared to vanish. Finally we were on our way. Next stop Blarney. This leg of the journey was a bit longer but eventually the train slowed and then stopped. A moment of confusion… this was the 3rd stop, but no Blarney marker. What to do?

My C.I.A. training said 'stay with the train'. We looked at each other, smiled, and got off. So here we are in Ireland in a huge grassy field. My training did actually help. I noticed the grass all stood 'tall' in the direction we had come from and the grass was matted down in the direction the train was going. So we followed the matted pathway for some time until we came to a turnstile. A turnstile in the middle of nowhere? A few minutes later we were introduced to a narrow road and within a few minutes heard the sound of a piano. We continued on toward the pleasant sound and within 50 feet or so, viewed a man playing the piano with three young children dancing and jumping to the rhythm of the music.

They waved at us as though we were a mile away. I pointed in the direction we were going "BLARNEY?" They smiled and in unison also pointed in the same direction. BLARNEY is not really a town unless three stores does a town make. Hardware, Apothecary and Soup Kitchen whose specialty was lentil soup. An older elf like gent joined us as we finished and inquired "Are ye' going to the castle"! It wasn't so much a question as it was a declaration. I said "yes" and he replied, "I thought as much" and directed us to the 'castle'. It was a short walk and on the way another 'Turnstile!' This time a woman with an apron held out her hand… We gave her some coins and moved on. The next site we saw was the ruins of an 800 year old castle.

*

"Are 'Ye' here to kiss the Stone?" I replied "Yes we are…and where are you?" Thru the mist he appeared. "Everyone wants to kiss the Stone, follow me." We quickly learned that one does not simply walk to the 'Stone', bend over and kiss it. No, no, no! Let me describe. Picture a casket on the floor with the top half closed and the bottom half open. One needs to lay on one's back and slither down under the 'Stone' (casket top), while the old gent grasps your ankles and raises them upward to help facilitate your descent under the 'Stone'. Who would go first? We played a quick game of Paper, Rock, Scissors and she lost so she would kiss the 'Stone' first. Fortunately her sun dress was ankle length.

*

While one is under the Stone, one might as well kiss it. If one is *claustrophobic*, one might want to be quick about it! Yes, she kissed it and then it was my turn. I must admit I could not stop laughing. All I had heard from my Irish relatives about the Blarney Stone and here I was on my backside about to pucker up and kiss a Stone. So I did it and the thought of a pocket wipe crossed my mind! Now it was time for the train ride back to CORK. 'The train has left the station' was an apropos phrase. Indeed it had departed. However, 'the Luck of the Irish' was with us. There was a bus to CORK! Five days later we were back in the U.S.A.

P.S. We eventually got married!

Author's note:

It has been said that SOCCER is the number one sport in the world. As a soccer referee for 40 years I agree. However, a ball, a field or school yard and usually 22 participants are required to create a match or game. Arguably the number one sport as well as the oldest toy in the world date back to 500 BC and that toy is?

CLUES

Keep it in your pocket! Tom Smothers! Don't know Tom? Double Bass Brother Dick? Walk the dog… Round the World, middle finger loop string… YES!!!!

YO-YO
(Good Job!)
YO-YO WORLD!

Senior Story from Friends: #3

I was born in Georgia in 1930, about the time Chicagoan Donald Duncan created his new company,

DUNCAN YO-YO

My father joined Donald shortly thereafter and for the next fifteen years my sister, my mom, dad & I, traveling almost exclusively by car, visited every state in the U.S.A. We also took trips to the Philippine Islands. All this travel was connected to the marketing and selling of the DUNCAN YO-YO. In America, baseball was THE sport! In the islands (as they were called) YO-YO was THE sport! They were the masters of the YO-YO. Thru the years thousands of men from the islands were brought to the U. S. as instructors.

*

Thousands of schools in the U.S. were treated to free YO-YO exhibitions by the YO-YO Masters. They would teach and demonstrate the 'magic' of the YO-YO. They held contests which encouraged students to display their skills. Prizes such as Schwinn Bikes were awarded for the student with the best YO-YO skills. I was told millions were sold and I'm sure dad made a lot of money, because each summer when schools were not in session, we traveled to Hawaii. During those years my sister and I attended two or three new schools every year. I'm not sure about my sister, but I love meeting new people. I continue to meet new people and have never stopped traveling. This year is my 80th Birthday. Husband and I will party
In Hawaii !

SENIOR GROUP MOMENTS!

On the 12 ft. bench in front of our townhouse complex, many owners daily gather for <u>W</u> & <u>W</u> (Wine & World Updates)! We also welcome other townhouse owners and their dogs. Polly and her dog 'Muffin' are regulars and on this day are accompanied by a man and his dog. As they enter our space Polly says, "Joey, I'd like you to meet Byron and while extending my hand to the owner, Polly says, Ah…"Byron is the dog!"

<u>**Speaking of Dogs!**</u> It is now 84 degrees and even though the heat in our pool will not ignite until May, I decided to 'go for it'. No Diving! (as usual, I did) As I skimmed the pool bottom, I notice strange settled 'lumps'. My mind screamed CRAP! ... Exactly what it was!

'THE BIG GUYS'

Being somewhat successful in Show Business, E & C often met and 'hung' with the big guys! We spent time with all of these senior citizens including the younger, but soon to be Medicare crowd. These are people who in some small manner had an influence on all our lives.

JOHNNY CARSON: The best ever at what he did. E & C (EDMONDS & CURLEY) made 3 appearances on the Tonight Show! Our first appearance with Johnny was memorable because after the show we made our way to his desk to thank him and at that moment he *Froze*...staring beyond us into the audience...one lone figure was making her way to the stage. I turned and said, "Oh, that's my wife." Johnny was the best ever, but I'll never forget that fearful look!

ED MCMAHON !

If you know who Ed was, then you know what he did…he Laughed! He laughed a lot! If you at home watching Johnny did not know when to laugh, Ed was your cheerleader. I met Ed a few years ago at a Comedy conference in Las Vegas. He was sitting at a round table for 10 and I said, "Mr. McMahon my name is Joey Edmonds. I was half of the Comedy Team EDMONDS & CURLEY and we appeared with you and Johnny a few times." He responded, "The Doctors Routine." 'WOW' He was willing to talk but the chairs were taken, so I knelt down next to him and we continued to chat. Moments later, during a lull I said, "If you bless me now, I'll be going !"

That's the last time I heard him laugh!

CARL REINER !

CARL was the Tonight Show host for EDMONDS & CURLEY's first national network appearance that featured the <u>Doctors Routine</u>. I don't think it could have been done any better! After the show we talked with Carl for a few moments and it was obvious he enjoyed the routine. "Original and funny! I've never seen anything like it!" This was 1969 when there was no video. We eventually received a Kinescope, but thru the years it was lost. Probably with Curley's Bongo Drums. It was terrific and a few of us will remember it forever! In 1983 we taped our last TV appearance 'Evening at the Improv'! I approached Mr. Reiner and said, "Edmonds & Curley"! He pointed at me and said,"

"The Doctors Routine!

JAY LENO!

Truly, what you see is what you get. I'm sure Jay must have a few problems with others in this world, but there cannot be many. As Jay, Jerry, Freddie, Larry and others were developing their comedy chops, E & C were closing in on 500 College Concerts. One event in my life solidified my admiration for Jay. I lived in Chicago across from Lincoln Park for 26 years and son Grant and daughter Kate and I would kick the soccer ball around. One day I ran into an unmarked hole (aren't they all) and messed up my ankle. This was early May and E & C had their final 'gig' at the end of the week in Fredonia, NY an hour south of Buffalo. It was obvious I would not be onstage at SUNY Fredonia.

What to do? E & C had never missed a show. I called Thom and he suggested that new kid LENO as a replacement. Jay agreed to cover the show. I explained that it was only $500 for 30 minutes of comedy. He accepted and on Friday drove from Boston to Fredonia and back the same evening. Two days later I called and asked how the show went. "It was okay, only a dozen or so students." I asked if they gave him the check and he said, "Yeah, but I gave it back." I replied, "Jay it's not your fault only 12 people showed up, welcome to college comedy shows where students have no idea who you are!" I've often wondered if Jay returned other checks?

Welcome Home Jay Leno!

ANDY KAUFMAN !

Where does one start! During his early days at the original Improv in 'Hells Kitchen' at 44th & 9th in NYC, Andy would just appear! If approached with the word 'hello', he may or may not nod! I, being A.D.D., was able to enjoy "Mighty Mouse" and cheer him on to save the day, but the moment he started to read his book to the audience, I was out the door. 'Man on the Moon' the 1999 movie was the story of Andy's life starring Jim Carrey as Andy & Andy's alter ego, Tony Clifton. I thought Jim's characterization was right on. I had the pleasure of watching and listening to Andy while in a swimming pool of a West Hollywood rental. He engaged a very attractive 20 year old and totally immersed her in his philosophy of the day.

*

I floated just close enough to hear his creative B. S. Andy never actually got <u>in</u> the water, he just stalked her around the edges of the pool. He had her so under his 'spell' that much to my disappointment, she never got out of the water. Foreign Man was my favorite Andy character who became Latka Gravas in the TV series *Taxi!* Foreign Man, in addition to lip synching Mighty Mouse, would also do impressions. BAD impressions of various people including President Jimmy Carter. To close his 'show' Andy would turn his back to the audience, turn up the collar of his shirt, comb his hair and become ELVIS! A GREAT ELVIS. Even the real ELVIS loved Andy's Elvis!

RED SKELTON !

In 1978 at the annual NACA (colleges) convention in San Antonio, Texas, Red Skelton was the featured speaker. Mary Jo the chairman of the board, who is a bit of a character herself, and yours truly greeted him. As we walked thru the expansive hallway we were slowed down by a maid who apparently had not missed many meals. After staring at the moving backside in front of us, Red uttered "Dear Loordie"! Mary Jo and I immediately covered our mouths. "Two cats fighting in a sack!" Now losing control, I loudly said to Mary Jo "let's walk ahead of this guy"! AND we did! I remember glancing back watching and listening to Red laughing at his own humor which he did all his life!

Funny & Nice!

<u>DAVID FROST !</u>

Englishman David Frost is probably best known for his interviews with President Richard Milhous Nixon. He was also the host of The DAVID FROST SHOW! E & C were 1st time guests and on this occasion we had written a comedy cooking show routine titled SGT. CHOW. David came out to applause and welcomed all to 'A Record Breaking Show'. "To start our Show, please remove your record from the sleeve. (pause)…everybody have your record? OK, Let's break your record for the comedy team of E & C !" No applause, Just record smashing! After 2 minutes we stopped, while records were still being destroyed and left the stage.

Oh, it's very funny, NOW!

MERV GRIFFIN !

In 1969 E & C auditioned for the Merv Griffin Show and were excited when we received a call the next day inviting us to appear 10 days later. We had already done the Tonight Show and would once again be flying back to NYC from Oshkosh, WI. The Merv Griffin Show was not aired on the local TV channel (Green Bay) so we had no idea about the show. Ten days later we land in NYC and that evening we hail a cab on 7th Ave. Cabbie asks "Where to"? Thom says "Bitter End". Because of the Tonight Show we were invited to perform at the famous **Bitter End** Music & Comedy Club. We're chatting away and eventually the driver pulls over and says "Here we are." Silence… he had taken us to the bitter end of 7th Ave.

The next afternoon we arrived at the Studio which was an old theater with a marquee that said, Merv Griffin Show! We were led to an office filled with people and one jovial person asking questions and then it was time for our sound check. Our routine for this show was the dentist drilling bit which drove every audience 'crazy' because of the sounds and me the patient physically sliding to the floor! Lots of applause and as we sat on the couch realized that the jovial staff member earlier in the office was Merv Griffin! We had never seen his show. Years later I had a picture taken with Merv at Del Mar race track. I asked if he remembered E & C and he said, "Dentist drilling bit!" I was impressed!

CANDICE BERGEN !

Boston Legal was <u>the</u> TV show Lynn & I never missed. James Spader, 'Captain Kirk' & Candice Bergen! In the 70's Dick Cavett hosted a talk show that was an alternative to Johnny Carson. E & C made two appearances, but the first one I will never forget. Dick's first guest was the beautiful Candice Bergen dressed in the style of the 70's. It was obvious they knew each other and after the commercial break, it was our turn. After our comedy set we joined Dick and Candice at the desk/couch. Stage left to right: Dick, Thom, Joey & Candice. Dick is bantering with Thom while I sit next to Candice sneaking peeks at her. About the 4th peek I notice her eyes are closed. I peek again, still closed. And again! Odd memory!

Never missed Boston Legal!

CHICO & THE MAN

E & C first met Freddie Prinze at the NY Improv and maybe because we were already at the 'top' of the college market and somewhat father figures, 19 year old Freddie felt comfortable talking to us. Mostly Thom, who like Freddie, was quite a personality and very talented. I remember one show Freddie did at the Friars Club for all the retired comics, they loved this young kid! The last time we saw Freddie was at the L.A. Improv. As we were leaving to catch a night flight to Richmond, VA, in walks Freddie with an entourage! "Curley… Edmonds, where you guys going?" " University of Richmond!" The next afternoon at 5 pm in the motel, my phone rang and I heard Thom's voice. "Freddie did it! Damn it!"

Drugs & Gun ended it all!

JERRY SEINFELD!

Freddie, Jay, Andy, Larry, Jerry and a host of other new 'kids' were starting to make their mark in the world of comedy. Jerry was at the head of the pack. He wrote jokes based on what all of us experience. Years later after E & C departed the college circuit, Jerry proved to the Tonight Show audiences he had arrived. With the help of Larry David, he became a household name! A year or two later I was on the same commuter plane with Jerry to Lancaster, NY. We chatted until I bored him and finally he said, time to write! "Got to keep ahead of the New Turks!" He's still keeping ahead of the New Turks!

SEINFELD! The name tells the story!

LARRY DAVID !

In addition to his amazing sound effects, partner Thom Curley played piano…no lessons, he just played. Also Bongo Drums which mysteriously disappeared 30 years ago. Also, his 6 inch switch blade knife could be opened, thrown and quivering in a tree or wall within 3-4 seconds. In the bar area of the NY Improv Comedy Club, one could sit at the far end of the bar and 10 feet away was a wall. Thom 'Jim Bowie' Curley would often demonstrate his knife tossing ability to applause or Ooooo's or the shaking of heads from other comics. One night LARRY DAVID approached the wall as Thom let it fly! Twang! "DAMN YOU CURLEY!"

Think About It

No SEINFELD!!!   No CURB!!!

JOHN DENVER !

I first met John in Minneapolis when Projects IV had a showcase for colleges that featured E & C as well as musical acts. One of the new acts was a Texas kid who had a very distinctive voice. Years later this 'kid' was to Star in a movie with George Burns -"Oh God"! John Denver songs like 'Leaving On A Jet Plane' 'Take Me Home Country Roads', 'Annie's Song,' and others became hits! E & C opened his concerts many times. One memory was Iowa State University where I sang harmony with him. The outfit he wore that evening I christened cowboy 'chaps'! His enthusiasm for life was like a little kid. Every once in a while I'll put on a John Denver CD and recall! One critic called him "A One Note Singer"

But, what he could do with that note!

STEVE ALLEN !

whim-si-cal; 1- Having eccentric ideas; capricious.   2 –Oddly constituted; fantastic; quaint.

Met Steve Allen only one time in Vegas at a Comedy Seminar. I was one of 10 at a round table during lunch. May I add the word cackle to his whimsical category? Steve Allen did not laugh, he cackled! Steve laughed at anything you did or said if it was funny. An older comic at the table never said a word, but with a dead-pan nod of the head, or roll of the eyes, or audible grunt unseated Steve to the floor. Of course it became contagious and very little food was consumed. All Steve's music and all his humor!

Arguably the best!

JONATHAN WINTERS !

Jon as we were told to call him, was ushered into the Edmonds life because of "Buzz & Joey"- Buzz being my singing partner prior to E & C. Because of 14 years with Thom, I was able to connect with Jon. It was Buzz's sister Marsha and husband Wes who were friends with Eileen and Jon. Once a year Buzz & Andrea would visit and I would dust off the guitar & banjo and the Edmonds would motor to Santa Barbara. Buzz, Marsha, Joey and occasionally Andrea and some other guest would join in. Jon would then create a story. One story had no ending even though he continued on searching for a finish. He abruptly morphed into his little boy Chester (pause) "Chester says THE END."

MIKE DOUGLAS SHOW!

Mike's show was taped in Philadelphia in front of an audience of mostly older ladies with their shopping bags. Mike was a regular guy and really liked us. We were invited back eleven times and after the first couple of times we just showed up and did our thing. There was a plethora of actors, singers, directors and other comedians. E & C were always treated like family. Our introduction for each show our intro was: "We never know what they're going to do, please welcome EDMONDS & CURLEY!
We would be funny and then cab it to the train station and be back in NYC before dark. Our eleventh appearance was a little different. Wife Lynn and Judie (our maid of honor a few years earlier), joined us.

*

  We wrote a new routine titled "CAMP FOR SHUT-INS!" starring 'Counselor Bob' & 'Camper Joey' for our next Mike Douglas spot in two weeks. The week prior we spent in Grand Forks, ND at a music club in the Westward Ho Motel. We planned on polishing this new material on our flights from NYC to Grand Forks and back, as well as 12 performances on stage. INNOCENCE! This routine was based on innocence because it was 'loaded' with double entendres and even though 'Counselor Bob' could be a 'naughty' counselor, camper Joey must be pure. We finally performed it on stage and the lines seemed to work well; however, the audience was not buying the innocence. They searched for the 'blue' immediately.

For the next 11 shows we wrestled with changes, attitude, improvisation & restraint. The restraint was mostly needed from Thom, but how does one coerce a real comedy artist like Thom not to go for the laughs. My problem was containing my innocence while Thom had the audience laughing.. at the wrong script. We went on like this for the rest of the week. We knew the routine, but the delivery was never quite correct. On the plane we continued…what…what…? Except for the doctors surgery gowns worn on our 1st Tonight Show, we never had costumes. Humm? 'Counselor Bob'? 'Camper Joey'? <u>Knee Length Boy Scout Uniforms</u>! We arrived in NYC and found two short sleeve/short pants BOY SCOUT OUTFITS!

On Wednesday Thom, Joey, Lynn & Judie arrived in Philadelphia and taxied to the Mike Douglas Show. Hello Fred, Hello Mary, Hello Band Leader. I escorted Lynn and Judie to the audience and joined Thom in our dressing room. Mike poked his head in "Got something special today?" "Yes we do Mike", I replied. The guests today were director Otto Preminger and actress Elke Sommer. (nice company)

 We have our sound check …we'll be using the BOOM mike plus wireless hand held for Thom because of his sound effects. 30 minutes later, "SHOW TIME"! We are dressed in our Boy Scout outfits and rearing to go. Mike is getting some kind of award and the dominantly female audience is loving it.

Mike brings out Otto for 10 minutes and then a commercial break. Elke Sommer (who is gorgeous) is introduced and they banter for 10 and another commercial break. and then, "We never know what these guys are going to do, please welcome EDMONDS & CURLEY! There is no band playing us on because we 'in our freshly minted Boy Scout outfits' provide our own music. "Da dad a…Da Da DaDa Da" as we introduce 'Counselor Bob' & 'Camper Joey' to the audience. Almost immediately we have the 'Mel Brooks watching Springtime for Hitler' audience'. It was 4 minutes of silence. We finish, bow like any happy boy scouts and leave. Before we can get to our dressing room, the director instructs us "to change clothes and give us a funny bit!"

We changed and again Mike repeated the words, "We never know what these guys are going to do, please welcome EDMONDS & CURLEY!" We did our Cop & Drunk driver bit which actually worked quite well. Some laughter, but we had not rehearsed the finish with the band, so there was a moment of silence before playing us off! That ended the show. I looked over at Otto and Elke who were looking at the floor. In fact I saw no eye balls from anyone! We departed ASAP for the last time as it turned out, had a few drinks and boarded the train to NYC. It was then that Lynn informed us the award Mike Douglas received was:

Boy Scout Father of the Year!

H I M

Whether positive or negative, the public figures I visited in the previous 24 pages had an influence on my life and I'm guessing many of yours. There is one person who I can guarantee has had a positive influence on the lives of every American in the past 60 years. E & C made 50 appearances on various talk shows in the almost 15 years we were a team and with one exception, each was a success.

    One of those shows featured a man who changed the face of our nation. During his segment on the show he spoke lovingly about his wife Rachel who was a nurse. I remember how enthralled the studio audience was being in his presence. After the show HE and E & C were escorted to a limo.

*

In the limo I told HIM I had a degree in nursing and the conversation was off and running. He asked how Thom (who was up front with the driver making him laugh…) and I formed the Comedy Team. I mentioned that three months of my nurses' training took place at Children's Hospital in Milwaukee. There was a female nurses' party and of course I was in attendance. I met this 6' 5" comic telling stories with 'sound effects' that created laughter for most of the night! Seven years later we became:

E & C ~ EDMONDS & CURLEY!

HE asked where I was born and I said Oshkosh and like everyone else in the world, he said "Oshkosh B'gosh". We chuckled and I mentioned that years ago, until I arrived at Fort Leonard Wood Missouri for Army Basic Training, I had never met anyone who was not caucasian. He gave me a wry smile and said, "You and millions more." A few minutes later we clasped hands and I departed. Two years later HE passed on. Many years later I refereed an AYSO soccer match adjacent to the famous Rose Bowl in Pasadena, and the field I refereed on?

JACKIE ROBINSON FIELD!

THANKS TO ALL OF YOU!

THOM CURLEY…Love Ya!

~ Jason Wilber for your 'Lazy Afternoon' CD which for 100's of hours soothed my old brain enough to write this!
~ Actress Judith Drake & Poet Dale J. Bilek for your amazing editing!
~ Joe Spereno who said 'that's the title!
~ My Gumba, Ray Juliano!
~ YO-YO Gloria ~ CIA Agent Ken
~ 'Utah' Jim Keneston.
~ Officer Larry
~ Cyclist Michael
~ Roger 'Picnic' Franzen
~ All others who gave me 2 or 3 word comments I may have incorporated!

Isn't this Fun !

NACA

National Association for Campus Activities!

Lifetime Membership Award!

Thank You

APCA

Association for the Promotion of Campus Activities!

Lifetime Achievement Award!

Thank You

www.ingramcontent.com/pod-product-compliance
Lightning Source LLC
Chambersburg PA
CBHW060845050426
42453CB00008B/841